Prayer and Meditation

Finding Comfort, Hope, and Purpose in the Midst of Your Storm

Joan M. Blake

Key to Life Publishing Company

Prayer and Meditation:
Finding Comfort, Hope, and Purpose in the Midst of Your Storm

Published by Key to Life Publishing Company
P.O. Box 190971
Boston, MA 02119
www.keytolifepublishingcompany.com

Table of Contents

Table of Contents

Table of Contents

Preface

Are you finding that your life is going in circles and that you are constantly struggling with life's issues? Have struggles in your past left you emotionally stranded and dealing with fear, anxiety, loneliness, guilt, anger, unforgiveness, resentment, or procrastination? Do you find that you are in need of a measure of strength and courage as you struggle to discipline and yet love your children, deal with your co-workers or your boss at the office, or handle any one of the hundreds of daily troubles that confront you?

Prayer and Meditation: Finding Comfort, Hope, and Purpose in the Midst of Your Storm is written for men and women in every walk of life who need tools to help them deal with problems in their daily lives and find comfort, hope, and purpose in the midst of their storms. This book is a collection of letters to the Lord that I have recorded in my journals over the years during my own struggles. I have written this book to edify God and to encourage you to persevere through rough times. Jesus Christ is the answer to all of the obstacles we face on our life's journeys. God promises never to leave or forsake us (Jos.1:5). When we entrust Him with our burdens, we find peace and rest (Phil. 4:6-7). We are overcomers because of Jesus' sacrificial death on the cross (Gal. 2:20).

This book is divided into five sections. The first section deals with affirmation. I wanted to share with you some insights about God's kindness, love, compassion, and faithfulness that I have experienced over the years. Ultimately, I would like you to be convinced that God is eager to heal us from our past and help us to live renewed and abundant lives. The second section deals with thanksgiving—thanking God for His love, for what He has already done, and for what He continues to do. John 3:16 tells us that God sent His only Son to die for us so we could have eternal life. In this section, I thank God for sending Jesus to bring salvation. The third section deals with meditation. I feel that as we thank God, we enter into a time of meditation on how great He is. Here I have shared thoughts in the form of poems or prose from my journals that represent what I was experiencing at the time. The fourth section consists of original prayer requests taken from my journals, while the fifth section consists of prayers that I have created for readers who may have needs other than those I addressed in my journals, such as those requiring medical, psychiatric, or counseling intervention. Prayer in these cases is an effective healing tool when used in combination with traditional treatment methods. The list of prayers in this prayer book is by no means exhaustive, so I have included blank lines within the additional prayers for you to include your own prayer requests. When you pray, believe that you have received what you have asked God for.

In this book, I have described my feelings during difficult times and how I had to reach out to God for strength. My journey through those difficult and yet enjoyable years has brought me closer to God than ever before. When I look back, I definitely see the hand of God upon my life. Without God, I would still be filled with unforgiveness in my heart, but because of God's grace and mercy, I have been filled with forgiveness and joy.

I have dedicated this book to my entire family: my husband, Carl, our sons, Tony and Rese, and our daughters, Monique and Jo-An.

I thank my husband, Carl, for his love and support. He has stood by my side and encouraged me to fulfill my dreams as a writer. Without his immense help with our daughter, Jo-An, I would not have been able to create this prayer book. I also thank him for giving me the insights for the subject index.

Tony, Rese, Monique, and Jo-An have been a great blessing to me. I rejoice over what God has done in their lives, and I thank them for the kindness and love that they have shown to me over the years.

I also want to acknowledge Renée Bergeron for her expertise in designing the cover and doing the layout for the book and also Ruth Hawk for her assistance with copyediting the book and making suggestions.

I have complied with my family's wishes to use middle names for our daughters and nicknames for our sons in order to preserve their privacy.

I hope that as you read this book, it will not only bring you peace, but will also increase your faith in the very God who longs to be in the center of your life and have a personal relationship with you through His Son, Jesus Christ.

Section: 1

Letters of Affirmation

No. 1
God Can Be Trusted

December 27, 1983 (Three months after giving birth to my daughter Jo-An, I underwent surgery.)

As I await surgery,
I identify with the Lord.
He sacrificed Himself for my
Salvation.[1]

Lord, I trust You
With my whole heart and soul.
I know You will see me through
So that I can be with my family.

You have blessed me with
A wonderful family.
I love You, Lord and Savior;
I love You,
Because You first loved me.[2]

---

[1] 1 Peter 2:24
[2] 1 John 4:19

No. 2
God Is Able

April, 1984 (I was tired and drained from caring for our four children, including a seven-month-old baby, and doing numerous household chores.)

I will overcome my difficulties,
Because God is fighting my battles.[3]
God is working in me,
Birthing patience in me,
And teaching me
How to show love to those
Who do not show love to me.

God is able,
Even if I am weak and unable.
He loves me so much
That He sent His Son
To die on the cross to save me
And give me life.[4]
The Gospel is true;
Light has come into the world.[5]

---

[3] 2 Chronicles 20:15
[4] 1 Peter 2:24; Romans 5:8-9
[5] John 3:19

No. 3
God Is on My Side

December 15, 1983 (Three months after giving birth to Jo-An, our youngest, and two weeks before my surgery, I sought God often in prayer and told Him exactly how I felt.)

I have grown weary of circumstances
That have made me unhappy;
However, God is on my side.
What can anyone do to me?[6]

I must be decisive and not fear.
God has promised a way out of darkness
Into His marvelous light,[7]
If I trust in Him.[8]

---

[6] Hebrews 13:6

[7] 1 Peter 2:9

[8] Hebrews 11:6

No. 4
God, You Are My All in All

May 31, 1990 (I felt God's presence in the midst of dealing with so much at home. I became very transparent, asking God to guide me, protect our family, and for His help in general. He gave me the guidance I needed during those difficult years.)

I praise You, God, and I magnify Your name,
For You alone are Holy.[9]
Lord, I feel Your presence,[10] even on this journey,
Where I experience frequent valleys and mountains.
I will not forget that You are with me,
That You love me,
And that Your Son Jesus, died on the cross for me.[11]
You promise to do a new thing in my life.[12]
You wait patiently for me to open the door of my heart,
So You can come in and sup with me.[13]
You are never tired of my endless prayers.

---

[9] Leviticus 19:2
[10] Exodus 33:14
[11] Romans 5:8
[12] Isaiah 43:19
[13] Revelation 3:20

You are my Counselor, my Savior, and my Comforter.[14]
You are all that I need;[15]
You are my sufficiency.[16]
You know all my desires.[17]
You are an Omnipotent, Omniscient, and Omnipresent God.[18]
You are blessed forever.[19]

You forgive sins.[20]
You are the Door by which I enter and am saved.[21]
You are the Way, the Truth, and the Life.[22]
You are my all in all.[23]

---

[14] Isaiah 9:6; Luke 1:47; John 14:16

[15] Philippians 4:19

[16] 2 Corinthians 12:9

[17] Psalm 139: 1-4

[18] Psalm 66:7; Psalm 139:16; Psalm 139:7-8

[19] Matthew 21:9

[20] Mark 2:7

[21] John 10:9

[22] John 14:6

[23] 1 Corinthians 15:28

No. 5
God, You Are My Strength and My Shield

May 10, 1990 (I was driving to Cape Cod, MA, for my annual personal retreat. It was very windy that day, and my car was swaying. I was a bit uneasy, as I do not particularly enjoy driving long distances.)

Even though I walk through the valley
Of the shadow of death,
I will fear no evil, for You are with me.[24]
Your grace is sufficient for me.[25]
I can do all things through Christ,
Who strengthens me.[26]

Thank You, God, for a safe journey
In spite of the fierce wind.
I love You and praise You, God;
You are my strength and my shield.[27]

---

[24] Psalm 23:4
[25] 2 Corinthians 12:9
[26] Philippians 4:13
[27] Psalm 28:7

No. 6
God, You Are My Hope in the Midst of Despair

December, 2001 (I felt lonely, but I was not alone, for God was with me.)

I extol You, Father,
Mighty King, above the heavens, and King over all the earth![28]
Oh, how much I praise and thank You for Your everlasting love.[29]
Thank You for blessing me with peace this week.[30]

I trust You with my life.[31]
During rough times, You make a way out for me.[32]
How I love You, Lord!
I can depend on Your love for me
Even when I am experiencing hate.[33]
When I experience sorrow, You give me joy.[34]
In the midst of turmoil, I can experience Your peace.[35]
When I am weak; You are strong.[36]
You give me hope in the midst of despair.[37]

---

[28] Psalm 47:7; Deuteronomy 10:14
[29] Jeremiah 31:3
[30] Luke 1:79
[31] Job 13:15
[32] 1 Corinthians 10:13
[33] Romans 8:35-37
[34] John 16:20; Romans 5:3-5
[35] John 16:33
[36] 2 Corinthians 12:9
[37] Psalm 42:5

No. 7
God, You Are Powerful and Mighty

March, 2002 (I sought the Lord in many areas in my life. I poured my heart out to Him.)

Holy God,[38]
I worship You.
I praise You;
I magnify You.
I extol You, King of kings and Lord of lords.[39]
I love You, because You first loved me.[40]
I will forever be grateful for Your love.
Lord, God, You are powerful and mighty.[41]

---

[38] Psalm 99:5
[39] 1 Timothy 6:15; Revelation 19:16
[40] 1 John 4:19
[41] Deuteronomy 10:17

No. 8
God, Be Glorified, This Day, and Forever!

October, 2002 (I had undergone a difficult medical test.)

My Lord and my God,[42]
My help in the time of trouble,[43]
How I reverence Your name, my Savior![44]
I cast my burdens before You,
And You heard me and delivered me from all my fears.[45]
I depended on You for strength,
And You, only You, were my source of strength.[46]
You are my sufficiency.[47]
You provide me with abundant joy[48] and unending love.[49]
You teach me to be patient and wait on You.[50]
You turn my weeping into dancing.[51]
God, be glorified, this day and forever.[52]

---

[42] John 20:28
[43] Psalm 46:1
[44] Isaiah 45:21; 1 Timothy 1:1; 2 Peter 1:1
[45] Psalm 34:4
[46] Psalm 28:7
[47] 2 Corinthians 12:9
[48] Psalm 43:4
[49] Jeremiah 31:3
[50] Psalm 37:7
[51] Psalm 30:11
[52] Psalm 86:9

No. 9
God, Remember Me

January 2002 (I had a panic attack; I felt that I was dying.)

Father,
You said that Your yoke is easy and Your burden is light.[53]
You remind me that only You have the power to deliver me.[54]
So, I trust You with my burdens,
For they are too heavy for me to carry.[55]
I depend on You, Lord, for all of my needs.[56]
Your grace is all that I need.[57]
God, remember me,
For You are my help.[58]

---

[53] Matthew 11:30
[54] Psalm 18:2; Psalm 144:2
[55] Matthew 11:28
[56] Philippians 4:19
[57] 2 Corinthians 12:9
[58] Psalm 46:1

No. 10
I Can Do All Things

April 2, 1992 (I was experiencing fear of the unknown, because there were so many decisions to be made around family and finances. I realized that I had to release my burdens to God and not take matters into my own hands.)

Father,
I know that all things are possible with You.[59]
I give You my heart.
I place all the details of my life into Your hands,
For You bear my burdens.[60]
I can do all things through Christ,
Who strengthens me.[61]

---

[59] Luke 1:37
[60] Psalm 68:19
[61] Philippians 4:13

No. 11
I Will Forever Be Grateful

October, 2002 (I was grateful for a benign biopsy.)

O Lord God,
I praise You this morning for being my God,[62]
My refuge in the time of trouble,[63]
My true witness,[64]
The horn of my salvation,[65]
My great King,[66]
My Creator, and friend.[67]
I stand as a testimony to Your divine intervention
In the lives of Your people,
And a proof of Your great love[68] and faithfulness.[69]
You guide and instruct me through Your Word.[70]
You make a way for me.[71]
You care for me[72] and preserve my life.[73]
I will forever be grateful to You.

---

[62] John 20:28; Psalm 18:2; Psalm 5:2
[63] Psalm 46:1
[64] Revelation 3:14
[65] Psalm 18:2
[66] Psalm 5:2
[67] Isaiah 40:28; John 15:13-14
[68] Ephesians 2:4; 1 John 3:1
[69] Psalm 36:5; Psalm 119:90
[70] Psalm 119:105
[71] 1 Corinthians 10:13
[72] 1 Peter 5:7
[73] Psalm 121:7-8

No. 12
I Will Tell Others of Your Greatness

December, 2002 (I was reflecting on God's grace and praising Him for what He had done and continues to do in my life.)

My Lord and my God, my Redeemer, my Rock, and my Salvation,[74]
I worship and praise You for who You are.
You are the Creator of heaven and earth.[75]
You are El Shaddai, the great I AM,[76] the Mighty God,[77]
And the Holy One.[78]
By Your might, You turned the Red Sea into dry ground
For the Israelites to walk over.[79]
You fed Your people with manna in the desert.[80]
You led them by a pillar of cloud by day
And a pillar of fire by night.[81]
You shut the mouths of lions.[82]

---

[74] John 20:28; Psalm 19:14; Psalm 18:2
[75] Jeremiah 32:17
[76] Exodus 3:14
[77] Deuteronomy 10:17
[78] Psalm 99:5
[79] Exodus 15:19
[80] Exodus 16:35
[81] Exodus 13:21
[82] Daniel 6:22

You fed the hungry,[83] healed the blind,[84]
And raised Lazarus from the dead.[85]
You sent Your Son, Jesus, to die in my place
So that I could obtain eternal life.[86]
I will go to the far ends of the world and proclaim Your greatness.

---

[83] Mark 6:35-41; Matthew 15:32-37; Luke 9:12-17

[84] Mark 8:23-25

[85] John 11:38-44

[86] John 3:16

No. 13
I Am Re-establishing My Faith in Jesus

July 7, 1990 (While I thanked God for my many blessings, I was anxious about my health during this period. I was not seeing myself as needing to be changed and molded. God used Isaiah 41:10, Isaiah 42:6, and Isaiah 43:7, 16, 25 to show me that it wasn't what I was going through that mattered; what mattered most was my relationship with Jesus Christ and the love He has for me.)

By faith, I believe
That Jesus died and rose again,[87]
And that He is sitting at the right hand of God, the Father,[88]
Making intercession for me.

By faith, I believe
That Jesus is my forerunner,[89]
And that He is the way to eternal life.[90]
He is my rock, my fortress, and my deliverer.[91]
He helps me walk with confidence.[92]
He fights my battles.[93]
He walks and talks with me.[94]

---

[87] Romans 6:4
[88] Acts 2:33
[89] Hebrews 6:20
[90] John 14:6
[91] Psalm 18:2
[92] Proverbs 3:26; Psalm 71:5
[93] 2 Chronicles 20:15
[94] Deuteronomy 5:24

By faith, I believe
That as I forgive others
And ask for forgiveness myself,
That God will forgive all of my sins.[95]

By faith, I believe
That anything I ask
According to my Father's will, I will receive.[96]
I ask in faith, not doubting.

Father,
By faith, I believe
That You are using this season of my life
To teach me humility.
By faith, I rest in You[97] and trust You with my life.[98]

---

95 Matthew 6:14-15
96 1 John 5:14
97 Matthew 11:28
98 Psalm 27:1

No. 14
I Resolve to Walk by Faith

January 2, 1992 (The prior month, December 1991, I had been asking for God's direction on my vocation, for help for my immediate family, for God to forgive and deliver me from an unclean heart and to renew my mind. He used Isaiah 40:31 to minister to me. What followed were my resolutions.)

Today, God, I resolve to walk by faith and not by sight,
Believing in You and Your divine Word.
I will not fail or be discouraged, for You are with me
And have not forsaken me.[99]
I resolve to follow Your leading and guidance
As You bring me to a new place in my life.[100]
I will trust in Your mercy and faithfulness[101]
As You carry me through my life journey.[102]

---

[99] Deuteronomy 31:6; Joshua 1:5

[100] Isaiah 43:19

[101] Psalm 145:8; 1 Corinthians 1:9

[102] Isaiah 46:4

No. 15
You Left Footprints to Prove That You Carried Me

November, 2002 (Following my surgical procedure in October 2002, I met with the surgeon, who explained that my situation needed special care, and that concerned me greatly. The same day, I wrote this letter.)

My Father, my Lord and my God,[103]
I adore You this morning,
And I give You praise and honor that is fitting for You only.

You have watched over my life.[104]
You have healed all my diseases[105]
And have kept me alive.
You have continually worked with and through me.
You carry me[106] through the storms of life,
For I see the footprints where You have treaded while carrying me.

---

[103] John 20:28
[104] Psalm 121:7
[105] Psalm 103:3
[106] Isaiah 46:4

No. 16
Jesus Is the Way

January 11, 2005 (I had been going through struggles with Jo-An, who is mentally challenged. Every successful step that I made was because of Jesus watching over me.)

I have been going through ups and downs,
But I prove that God is faithful.
Through the storms,
I have come to know my Savior and Lord in a unique way.
He calms my fears and soothes my pain;
I can't help but say that He is the Way.[107]

---

[107] John 14:6

Section: 2

Letters of Thanksgiving

No. 17
Thanking God in All Circumstances

(On Saturday July 30, 1983, at the American Baptist Camp in Maine, I was pregnant with our fourth child and had to leave the Bible study to care for our boys, who were behaving selfishly and not wanting to share. Although I was upset in the morning, everything worked out well in the afternoon, as our children participated in a talent show, singing and playing the piano.)

Lord,
I thank You in all circumstances,
For You make all things work together for my good.[108]
I will remain steadfast in prayer,
Believing, and trusting, in You.

---

[108] Romans 8:28

No. 18
Thanking God for Relaxation and Meditation

(Thursday July 28, 1983, at the American Baptist Camp in Maine, I used that morning to relax and commune with God while my children were with their counselors doing arts and crafts.)

Dear Lord God,
Thank You for comforting me,
And causing me to relax,
And meditate on Your goodness toward me.[109]
Lord, You are wonderful[110] and faithful.[111]
You are a great God[112] and friend.[113]
Today, I meditate on Your love for me
And thank You for this relaxing time.

---

[109] Psalm 107:8
[110] Psalm 107:8
[111] 1 Corinthians 1:9
[112] Psalm 48:1
[113] John 15:13-14

No. 19
Thanking God for Using Others to Bless Me

September, 2002 (I was thinking about how God uses his Church, the many people that I have come in contact with over the years, and how they have blessed me through their love.)

Holy Father,
I bow before You.
You are great in the heavens and in the earth.[114]
I pay homage to You, dear God.
I glorify Your name this morning,
For Your name is greater than every other name.[115]
Thank You for opening my eyes this morning
And giving me the opportunity to enjoy a great day.
Thank You for using others to bless me.

---

[114] Deuteronomy 3:24
[115] Philippians 2:9

No. 20
Thanking God for His Unconditional Love

October, 2002 (While this month was trying because of the surgery I had, I was thankful for God's healing. We celebrated my husband's birthday five days before my surgery, and we had joy just seeing our daughter Jo-An and all of our family members happy.)

I praise You, Mighty God, Wonderful Counselor,[116]
My Redeemer,[117] my Crown,[118] and the lifter of my head.[119]
I praise and worship You this morning for being my Creator.[120]
Thank You for loving me just as I am.[121]
Thank You for giving me peace and joy,[122]
For providing for me,[123] for healing me,[124]
And for calling me out of darkness into Your marvelous light.[125]
You are forever assuring me that You are by my side
And that You will never forsake me.[126]
Thank You, Lord God, for Your unconditional love.[127]

---

[116] Isaiah 9:6
[117] Psalm 19:14
[118] Isaiah 28:5
[119] Psalm 3:3
[120] Isaiah 40:28
[121] Jeremiah 31:3
[122] Psalm 29:11; Nehemiah 8:10
[123] Philippians 4:19
[124] Psalm 30:2
[125] Psalm 18:28; 1 Peter 2:9
[126] Psalm 139:7; Joshua 1:5
[127] Jeremiah 31:3

No. 21
Thanking God for Longevity of Life

August, 2002 (I was especially joyful that I had joined a new church and participated in their Vacation Bible School. I was praising God for longevity of life, because He gave me the chance to be a part of a great body of believers.)

I come before You, Father,
In humble submission to Your authority
And awesome power.[128]
No one can take Your place in my life;
I owe my life to You.

I come to thank and praise You
For giving me longevity of life[129]
And for working everything out
According to Your will and purposes.[130]

---

[128] 2 Peter 1:3
[129] Psalm 91:16
[130] Ephesians 1:11

No. 22
Thanking God for All Things

December 10, 1991 (In October, I bombarded God with many requests, including a prayer to use me, to mold and shape me. I turned my prayer requests into thanksgiving.)

Thank You for Your greatness, Father.[131]
Thank You for lighting my lamp.[132]
Thank You for giving me the desires of my heart.[133]
Thank You for answering my prayers.[134]
Thank You for protecting me.[135]
Thank You for delivering me.[136]
Thank You for giving me strength.[137]
Thank You for Your grace, which is sufficient for me.[138]
Thank You for Your love and guidance.[139]
Thank You, God, for Your precious mercy[140]
And for Your righteousness.[141]
Thank You for all things, Father,
For all things work together for my good.[142]

---

[131] Psalm 147:5
[132] Psalm 119:105
[133] Psalm 37:4
[134] Psalm 91:15
[135] Psalm 46:1; Psalm 91:4
[136] Psalm 32:7; Psalm 34:4
[137] Philippians 4:13
[138] 2 Corinthians 12:9
[139] Jeremiah 31:3; Psalm 32:8
[140] Ephesians 2:4
[141] Psalm 145:17
[142] Romans 8:28

No. 23
Thanking God for His Care

September, 1990 (I wrote this prayer during our daughter, Jo-An's, 7th birthday).

Father God,
I praise You this morning,
For You are my light and my salvation.[143]
Although I face challenges in my daily life,
I shall not fear;
For You are making a way for me.[144]
Thank You for Your benefits[145]
And for Your total care of me.[146]

---

[143] Psalm 27:1

[144] 1 Corinthians 10:13

[145] Psalm 103:2

[146] 1 Peter 5:7

No. 24
Thanking God for Healing My Inner Spirit

August, 1985. (At Saco, Maine, at a healing service at an American Baptist family camp, I was overwhelmed with family and financial burdens.)

Thank You, God,
    For Your mercy and love,[147]
    For Your protection,[148]
    For Your guiding hands upon my life,[149]
    And for healing my inner spirit.[150]
Now, I have reasons for living,
Motivation to move forward,
And renewed love for my family.
Most of all, Lord, I can draw closer to You.

---

[147] Ephesians 2:4
[148] Psalm 91:4
[149] Psalm 32:8
[150] Psalm 147:3

No. 25
Thanking God for His Presence

May 15, 1986 (On Cape Cod, MA, during my personal retreat time)

Dear Lord,
Thank You for affording me this quiet time,
To seek You with my whole heart,
And to get to know You more.
You promise never to leave or forsake me.[151]
Thank You for Your presence, Lord.[152]

---

[151] Joshua 1:5
[152] Psalm 139:7-8

No. 26
Thanking God for Helping Me to Stand on His Promises

June 2002 (Every day was a challenge caring for Jo-An. God's grace sustained me, and because of His love, I made a decision to stand on His promises.)

Lord, God,
Thank You for Your sustaining power.[153]
Thank You for Your unconditional love,[154] Your care,[155]
And Your healing of my inner pain.[156]
Thank You that Your joy is my strength,[157]
And Your grace is sufficient for me.[158]
Thank You for Your protection from the power of the enemy.[159]
Thank You that I can stand on Your promises,
Regardless of the situations I face.

---

[153] Hebrews 1:3
[154] Jeremiah 31:3
[155] 1 Peter 5:7
[156] Psalm 147:3
[157] Nehemiah 8:10
[158] 2 Corinthians 12:9
[159] Psalm 91:3-7

No. 27
Thanking God for My Deliverance

July 2002 (God had spoken to me numerous times regarding the need to have faith and reminded me that He had not forgotten me and that my deliverance was on the way, so I began to rejoice.)

I come to You, Lord,
Not with tears of sorrow, but with tears of joy,
In anticipation of what You are about to do in my life.[160]
Thank You for giving me peace in the midst of my storm.[161]
Thank You for Your healing power.[162]
Thank You for delivering me from the distresses of life.[163]

---

[160] Jeremiah 29:11
[161] John 14:27
[162] Exodus 15:26
[163] Psalm 34:4

No. 28
Thanking God for His Revelation

January 5, 1992 (God was revealing that He had a plan for my life and that my calling was based on Luke 4:18.)

Thank You, God, for revealing, through Your Word,
Your greatness and Your Power[164]
To change my life and my circumstances.[165]
Your revelation provides guidance and strength for me.
Thank You for revealing Yourself as my Redeemer,[166]
The One who fights my battles,[167]
And the One who makes a way of escape for me.[168]

---

[164] Psalm 147:5
[165] Isaiah 61:1
[166] Isaiah 47:4
[167] 2 Chronicles 20:15
[168] 1 Corinthians 10:13

No. 29
Thanking God for His Love and Faithfulness

July, 2002 (I was constantly going before God. It seemed that everywhere I turned, there were roadblocks to my destiny. I listened as God revealed through Isaiah 40:31 and Matthew 11:28 that He would renew my strength when I waited on Him and would give me rest when I entrusted my burdens to Him.)

O my God, my Lord and my Savior,[169]
How I love You today!
You are worthy of all praise and glory.
I magnify You and exalt Your name,
My King, my Redeemer,[170] and my Deliverer.[171]
I thank You from the bottom of my heart
For Your love and mercy.[172]
Thank You for the faith You have given me.[173]
Thank You for Your love and faithfulness.[174]

---

[169] Isaiah 43:3
[170] Isaiah 44:6
[171] Psalm 18:2
[172] Ephesians 2:4
[173] Galatians 3:22
[174] Psalm 92:2

No. 30
Thanking God When I Feel Unworthy

July, 2002 (Being a caretaker, robbed me of energy, and, sometimes, I was unable to see God's hand on my life, until I began to thank Him in my situation.)

Dear Father,
I come to You in the beauty of Your holiness.[175]
I praise You for who You are, Lord.
Thank You for preserving my life[176]
And for giving me a future.[177]
Thank You, God, for giving me faith, hope, and love.[178]
Thank You, Father, that even when I feel unworthy of Your love,
I can go before You,
Because Your Son, Jesus, has already paid the penalty for my sins,
By dying on the cross.[179]

---

[175] Psalm 48:1
[176] Psalm 121:7
[177] Jeremiah 29:11
[178] 1 Corinthians 13:13
[179] Romans 5:8

No. 31
Thanking God for Jesus' Shed Blood

July, 2002 (Another letter of thanks to God for dying on the cross for me)

God,
I praise You on the mountaintop; I praise You in the valley.
I praise You in the morning; I praise You at noon.
All day long, I will sing praises unto You, Lord.
I cannot thank You enough
For sending Your Son, Jesus,
To die on the cross for my redemption.[180]

---

[180] Galatians 3:13-14

No. 32
Thanking God for His Word

July 23, 1987 (I was struggling internally, feeling lonely and rejected, but I was affirming God's love for me through His Word.)

Lord, God,
Thank You for Your divine Word,
Which is sharper than a two-edged sword.[181]
Thank You for Your Word
That is a lamp to my feet and a light to my path.[182]
Thank You that I can trust Your Word.[183]
Your Word increases my understanding
And gives me wisdom and knowledge.[184]
Your Word revives me and gives me hope.[185]
Thank You for Your life-giving, transforming Word.

---

[181] Hebrews 4:12
[182] Psalm 119:105
[183] Psalm 119:42
[184] Proverbs 2:6
[185] Psalm 119:49

No. 33
Thanking God for His Blessings

January, 2009 (I was thanking God for the times that He had healed members of my family and helped us in our difficult journey.)

Thank You, Lord, God,
For Your blessings, both small and great.[186]
Thank You for this life on earth.
Thank You for protecting my entire family from harm,
For healing us from sickness and emotional pain.[187]
Thank You that whether I live or die, I am Yours.[188]
Thank You for giving me faith to be an overcomer.[189]
Thank You that by Your grace I am saved,
Not by my works, but by Your gift.[190]

---

[186] Psalm 103
[187] Psalm 103:3-4
[188] Romans 14:8
[189] 1 John 5:4
[190] Ephesians 2:8

Thank You that no temptation is so great
That I cannot withstand it.[191]
You said, Lord, that You would make a way of escape
So that I can bear temptations.[192]

I thank You that Satan cannot steal my joy.[193]
I live by faith and not by sight.[194]
Thank You for the families with whom You have blessed me.
Thank You for Your provisions, Lord.[195]
Thank You for delivering me from my past. [196]

---

191 1 Corinthians 10:13
192 1 Corinthians 10:13
193 Jude 1:24
194 2 Corinthians 5:7
195 Philippians 4:19
196 Psalm 34:4

No. 34
Thanking God for Another Day

September 1, 1990 (A period of recognizing all that God had done for me and thanking Him for another day)

I praise and worship You, Father, for You are my God in whom I will trust.[197]

You said in Your Word that this is the day that You have made and that I should rejoice and be glad in it.[198]

Thank You for giving me a comfortable rest[199]and for allowing me to see another day.[200]

---

[197] Psalm 18:2
[198] Psalm 118:24
[199] Isaiah 32:18
[200] Isaiah 50:4; Psalm 3:5

Section: 3

Letters of Meditation

No. 35
My Baptism Is Drawing near

(Eve of my baptism, Spring, 1978)

Three days before Palm Sunday,
I lie on my bed, restless and unable to sleep
In the early morning hours.
I hear the sounds of the dogs trotting
And the baby in her crib playing,
And I declare, "Oh, what a beautiful morning!"

I resume my thoughts.
I feel the loving touch of Jesus
And sense the presence of the Holy Spirit.
I am thrilled with life.

Oh, what excitement I feel
On the eve of my baptism —
An excitement that I have never felt before!
Oh, what relief it is to know
That I have found a Friend forever!

No. 36
Put Your Confidence in God

December 1, 1983 (Three months after giving birth to my youngest child, Jo-An)

I feel like a little baby stripped of all my clothes,
Waiting for my mother to dress me.
I am in the middle of a desert,
Wanting to shout,
But no one will hear me.
I have decided to press on
Until I come to that joyful end.
I am able to do so
By putting my confidence in God.

No. 37
Have No Fear, for Jesus Is Near

July 22, 2000 (Financially stripped from having helped a friend whose motive was fraud)

I awake this morning with so much on my mind.
Jesus said, "I will take care of Your problems; stop being blind."
So I said, "Jesus, what do You want me to do?"
He said, "Praise me, and I will see You through.[201]
Have no fear;
For I am near."

I sat at the table to sup
And thought of all my problems.
Jesus reassured me
That I need not worry,
For He has placed me on top.
"Have no fear;
For I am near."

I thought of my pain,
But Jesus told me that after the storm,
There is gain.
"Do not worry; do not panic.
Have no fear;
For I am near."

---

[201] Psalm 18:3

I thought of how a friend betrayed me and took me in.
Jesus reminded me that He paid the penalty because of sin.
I thought of the grief, the loss of all that I had;
Jesus told me there was no reason to be sad.
"Have no fear;
For I am near."

I thought of how I would make it day by day.
Jesus told me, "Don't worry, I will provide the pay."
I looked around and realized I needed help.
My Master assured me I need not carry the load myself.
"Have no fear;
For I am near."

I said, "Lord, I have prayed for my daughter's healing.
It has been a long time, Lord."
He said, "Wait on me patiently,[202] and do not be bored.
Have no fear;
For I am near."

[202] Psalm 37:7

I have sinned and fallen short of Your glory.[203]
I have been feeling anxious and lonely.
But Lord, You have allowed me to be in this place,
So You alone can help me run this race.
        "Have no fear;
        For I am near."

I love You, Lord, for You have heard my cry.
You are helping me by and by.
You have not left me alone.
All my sins You said are foregone.
        "Have no fear;
        For I am near."

[203] Romans 3:23

No. 38
Jesus' Light Pierces through Dark, Dismal Failures

July 22, 2000 (I felt like a failure from having lost money to a friend, the discouragement of being weary from day to day, of not walking completely in my purpose, and of facing my son's imprisonment.)

I have learned from experience
That failure is inevitable to arrive at success.
I search my mind,
And within me, I find
          Dark, dismal failures.

In my home there is no help around;
I get discouraged and forget that Your help surrounds,
          Despite dark, dismal failures.

Among my children, there are some success stories,
Others not so good.
But with faith, all things stood,
          Despite dark, dismal failures.

My job is taking up my time,
But I refuse to give up the dime
          For fear of dark, dismal failures.

I have become anxious in my life,
Unable to understand the strife

That causes me to experience
Dark, dismal failures.

I struggle with being accepted;
I continue to feel rejected
And fear dark, dismal failures.

I desire to be free;
I can't seem to be.
My life seems so dampen;
However, blessings are about to happen,
Despite dark, dismal failures.

I wonder when I will come through;
My life seems so rough.
I can no longer stand alone;
That thought is foregone.
Jesus' light pierces through
Dark, dismal failures.

Jesus is my guide;
He rides the tide.
His anointing hands around me,
His guidance, strength, and love will see me through
Dark, dismal failures.

No. 39
Life Goes on, So Can I

July 23, 2000 (In order to live an abundant life, I realized that I had to forego the things over which I had no control and seek God to renew my mind.)

My heart is sad.
Why do I feel so bad?
        Life continues, and so can I.

The storm is passing by;
There is no need to sigh.
        Life continues, and so can I.

I am here to please my Master;
I am here to run this race faster.
        Life continues, and so can I.

The race is not for the swift,
Nor for those who make a rift.
        Life continues, and so can I.

I will never be the same
As long as I am in this game.
        Life continues, and so can I.

"I will look unto the hills from whence comes my help;"[204]
My help comes from Jesus Himself.
Life continues, and so can I.

[204] Psalm 121:1

No. 40
Jesus Is Mine

July 24, 2000 (Still feeling sad and disappointed that I put my trust in someone and was betrayed)

I call on Jesus all the time, especially in times of need.
Jesus provides the answer; His Word provides the feed.
Jesus calls His sheep to follow,
No matter how our minds are shallow.

In spite of your sin,
Jesus takes you in.
In whatever state you are,
Jesus takes you far.

You need not worry about your past;
Jesus calls first those who are last.[205]
You will find favor and rest,
As you humbly go through your test.

Jesus is your King;
Let those words continue to ring.
For His blood covers you,
And His love sees you through.

---

[205] Matthew 19:30

No. 41
When My Life Is Out of Control

July 25, 2000 (Difficulty getting my finances in order after being defrauded)

I feel lonely;
I forgot that praise is comely.
I feel blue;
Why? I don't have a clue.
I don't know what to do;
I don't know where to go,
Because my life is out of control.

I don't know the reason for my situation.
I feel like someone in litigation.
I feel lost,
Steered away from my post,
Because my life is out of control.

I have never felt so trapped.
It seems my life is mapped
To go in a certain way.
My Master is in control; I have to say,
Although my life seems out of control.

The way I feel
Causes me to kneel.
It forces me to trust,
Although I put up a fuss
When my life is out of control.

I can't see the road before me;
I can only trust there is a good future to be.
I can't envision God's plans for me;
I am human and unable to see,
Because my life is out of control.

I am up one day and down the next,
Although I read biblical text.
In my hopeless state,
I trust my fate
To the One who guides,
In whose bosom I hide,
When my life is out of control.

No. 42
Yield to the Holy Spirit

Sep. 3, 2000 (One month after attending a healing service where Jo-An was not healed from her mental condition)

The Lord heard my cry concerning my family.
He gave me strength to continue my fight,
And gave me rest from my toil.
I trusted Him for my deliverance
Regardless of how long it took.
I praised my God and got my relief.

I became available to my Lord
And ready to be made over.
As I became clay in His hands,
He worked in and through me.
He changed me, fashioned me,
And made me into the vessel
He wanted me to be.

I settled in His will
And trusted in His love and care,
And came to know God in a special way.

No. 43
I Love the Lord

Sep. 30, 2001 (As I continued to look to the Lord for my everyday needs, He showed me that He was my helper (Psalm 121), that I needed to be still and know that He is God (Psalm 46), and that He would always be with me.)

I love God,
For He has never left me.[206]
When I cried out to Him,
He helped me.[207]
He gave me joy when I sorrowed;[208]
He picked me up when I was weak.[209]
I love the Lord,
For He heard my cry.

---

[206] Joshua 1:5

[207] Psalm 138:3

[208] Isaiah 51:11

[209] 2 Corinthians 12:9; Psalm 40:2

No. 44
Lord, I Am Forever Yours

Nov. 7, 2001 (I was expecting to receive a subcontracting opportunity from someone to whom I was referred, but that did not happen.)

When the time of maturity had come,
I left my dwelling place
And came to a world
That I did not know.

I left the comfort of my mother's womb;
It was soft and cuddly,
And I could rest.
I could snuggle
And listen to the noise of her body,
Which made me feel secure.

As I grew up, I understood
That someday, somewhere, sometime,
I would come to know a Savior, Jesus, my Lord,
Who would give me the protection I needed.[210]

In times of difficulty,
I would call upon Him,
Morning, noon, or night,
And He would hear my cries.

---

[210] Psalm 91:4

I would nestle at His feet
And tell Him all that was on my mind.
His words of comfort were always one of a kind.[211]

In good times, I tended to forget my Maker,
Believing I was in control,
Until my life began to unravel.
I understood the Lord's purposes for my life
Amid hardships I endured.
He brought me peace more than I could imagine.[212]
I know for certain, Lord, I am forever Yours.

---

[211] Psalm 71: 21

[212] Ephesians 2:14

No. 45
I Am Tossed To and Fro

November 16, 2001 (I was deciding whether to end my leave and return to my job or extend my leave and care for our daughter Jo-An at home. Bills were piling up, but I had nowhere to send our daughter.)

I'm like a ship
Tossed to and fro.
The waters overflow,
And the winds blow.

The sea roars,
And the thunder is heard.
Jesus is my captain;
He commands the waters
And the winds to cease,
And calms the troubled ship.[213]

In times of storms,
He reminds me to stay calm.
My Master knows best
How to use storms as my test;
He teaches me how to conquer my fears
And trust in His care.[214]

---

213 Mark 4:39
214 Psalm 125:1

No. 46
I Can Overcome Hills and Mountains

January 7, 2002 (The day turned out to be extremely difficult for me when I took Jo-An to the hospital for her appointment. God assured me that all I needed to do was trust Him and not lean on my own understanding (Proverbs 3:5).)

Over the hills and mountains, I climb,
Persevering to see my Savior and to draw close to Him.
Sometimes I slip, sometimes I fall,
But He is always faithful to pick me up.[215]

He provides the hills and the mountains as challenges
To show me how excellent He has been to me.
He has shown me daily that the mountains I can overcome,
And the valleys I can be lifted from.

[215] Psalm 40:2

No. 47
Keep Your Eyes on Jesus

March 6, 2002 (For the past few days, I had sought God in prayer and praise, worked on writing the newsletter, and publishing it on the website. I continued to organize my personal journals and read the promises God made to me: to seek Him and find Him, not to look for affirmation from others but to trust Him in everything.)

You are in the midst of turbulence—
A raging storm.
The seas are roaring.
The waves are high.
        Keep your eyes on Jesus;
        He is all you need.

You can't see the light from afar.
All you see is the struggle that is near.
In the pain of darkness, you fumble;
In the light of success, remain humble.
        Keep your eyes on Jesus;
        He is all you need.

In the midst of the raging seas,
Seek the Lord, who says,
"Come unto Me."[216]
In the midst of the sinking ship,
I cry, "Master, save me, lest I slip."
        Keep your eyes on Jesus;
        He is all you need.

---

[216] Matthew 11:28-30

No. 48
God Has the Master Plan

April 4, 2002 (I had a talk with the Lord while I took a walk; I went to the library, and worked on my book. As a result, I had peace.)

I awake this morning to the light
Illuminating my window.
The skies are blue; the sun is bright,
And the air is fresh.
I owe it to my God and Savior;
He has the master plan.

I have zeal; I have life.
I can walk; I can run.
I can speak; I can scream.
I owe it to my God and Savior;
He has the master plan.

I can hop; I can dance.
I can jump; I can leap.
I can smile; I can laugh.
I can sing; I can shout.
I owe it to my God and Savior;
He has the master plan.

I can lie; I can roll.
I can stand; I can move.
I can hug; I can feel.
I can forgive; I can love.
I owe it to my God and Savior;
He has the master plan.

No. 49
Who Am I?

September 18, 2002 (God was speaking to me about being confident and strong. He told me to, "Rise from the ash heap and put on a garment of praise.")

I am your pillar; I am your post.
    You can lean on Me.
I am your shadow; I am your guide.
    You can follow Me.
I am your shield; I am your cover.
    You can trust Me.
I am Jesus; I am your Redeemer.[217]
    You can honor Me.
I am your joy; I am your crown.[218]
    You can praise Me.
I am your Master; I am your King.[219]
    You can glorify Me.
I am everything to you; I am yours.
    You can depend upon Me.
I am your sacrifice; I am the Resurrected One.
    You have salvation because of Me.[220]

---

[217] Psalm 19:14
[218] Isaiah 28:5
[219] Luke 17:12-13; 1 Timothy 6:15
[220] John 11:25; Romans 5:10

No. 50
I Am Washed in the Blood

September 19, 2002 (God revealed that His Son, Jesus, died so I could have life and that I needed to live with an expectation to receive all things from Him.)

When the storm hits home and I am unable to walk
Because the waters surround,
I depend on my Lord to carry me in His arms.
I am excited about my Savior.
I give Him my life and have no regrets.
He is my champion in this race;
I follow Him where He leads.
I am washed in the blood, no longer soiled in sin;[221]
My Master saw it fit to give me a new start again.

---

[221] 1 John 1:7

No. 51
Don't Cry

September 20, 2002 (I was overcome by Jesus' love for me as I listened to what He said to me.)

Do not cry, my daughter (my son).
I died and was resurrected to give you hope;[222]
I have wiped away all your tears.

Do not cry, my chosen one.
Everything will come to pass as I said it would.
Bear with Me; the time is at hand.

Do not cry, my beloved.
You are an overcomer because of my shed blood on Calvary.
My blood redeems, heals, and sets you free.[223]

Do not cry, my servant.
In due time, your troubles will pass,
And you will testify of my greatness.

Do not cry, my precious one.
I know what is best for you.
I know how to discipline you.
Leave your life to Me, for I care for you.[224]

---

[222] Romans 4:24-25; Romans 5:1-5

[223] Romans 4:24-25; Romans 5:1-5

[224] 1 Peter 5:7

No. 52
Reflect on God's Goodness

May 13, 1991 (I look back at my journals and realize that I was dealing with a lot of emotional issues and that God was taking me through the process of healing and bringing me to Himself.)

Father,
What a joy to go back over one year of writing
And see how I have grown spiritually.
I owe it to You, Lord, God,
And I give You the glory and praises for it.

You are doing great things in my life.[225]
You are forever walking with me through the valleys, [226]
Caring for me, and carrying me in the palm of Your hand.[227]

You have established my goings and given me songs of praise.[228]
These praises are to You, God, and to my Savior, Jesus Christ.[229]
I praise You, God, and I bless Your name forever.

---

[225] Psalm 71:19

[226] Psalm 23:4

[227] 1 Peter 5:7; Psalm 91:12

[228] Psalm 40:2-3

[229] Jude 1:25

No. 53
God Sees Me through

December, 2003 (One semester left before my graduation from seminary)

This semester has come to an end.
God, you have been wonderful to me.
Without Your help,[230] I could not have made it.
You gave me the strength and the guidance that I needed.[231]
You bore my problems,
And You gave me peace in the midst of my struggle.[232]
Oh how great You are, my Lord, my Savior, and my Redeemer.[233]

---

[230] Psalm 46:1
[231] Psalm 46:1; Psalm 32:8
[232] Psalm 68:19; John 14:27
[233] Isaiah 49:26

No. 54
Enjoy the Beauty of the Ocean

July 19, 2003 (This was the final day of my vacation in Maine with my two daughters; we sat at the beach for an hour and a half before heading home.)

On this bright Saturday morning,
The sun is shining on the water.
People are swimming, boating,
Surfing, or walking around,
Hoping to find shell pieces in the sand.
Others are sitting on chairs eating
And chatting with family members and friends,
Under umbrellas that sway in the wind.
They watch their children
As they play and build sandcastles.

There is peace here.
There is joy here.
God's presence resonates through the wind,
Leaving a refreshing, cooling, and calming sea breeze.
God speaks through the noise of the waves
That creates laughter and joy,
As families eagerly wait to ride the tide.
God smiles through the shining sun
As it overshadows the beach filled with people
Waiting to get a glimmer from its radiance.
God's skies gleam over the seemingly blue waters,
Displaying the beauty of His creation.

Section: 4

Letters of Prayer

No. 55
Prayer When Feeling Lonely

Morning of July 26, 1983 (I was pregnant with our fourth child and attending the American Baptist Church Camp, in Maine, alone with our three children. God was testing me to see whether I would rest in Him or give up.)

God sets the lonely in families,
he leads out the prisoners with singing;
but the rebellious live in a sun-scorched land (Psalm 68:6 NIV).

Father, God,

I love You and will not forget Your Word or Your promises, even in these times of testing.

I confess and repent of my feelings of emptiness and loneliness, Lord.

Please help me to understand Your love for me, regardless of the situation I face.[234] Soothe and comfort me in my loneliness, Lord, so that I do not feel like giving up. Lord, heal my lonely heart and set me free, I pray, in Jesus' name, Amen.

---

[234] Romans 8:35

No. 56
Prayer for My Extended Family

August 9, 1983 (Nearing our daughter's birth)

....Finally, all of you, be like-minded, be sympathetic, love one another, be compassionate and humble (1 Peter 3:8 NIV).

Father,
I love You and praise You.
You put everything into perspective
For those who trust in You.
Lord, God, I pray that my extended family
Will grow in love and unity,
And have You, Lord, as the head of their lives.
In Jesus' name, I pray, Amen.

No. 57
Prayer for Several Needs

March 1, 1986 (In my prayer, I wanted God to help and direct my family and me and fill me with His peace.)

When you pass through the waters,
I will be with you;
and when you pass through the rivers,
they will not sweep over you.
When you walk through the fire,
you will not be burned;
the flames will not set you ablaze
(Isaiah 43:2 NIV).

Lord, God,
My strong tower and my strength,[235]
I praise You and magnify Your name.
Thank You for Your love and comfort this day.[236]
I confess that I feel overwhelmed.
I repent and ask Your forgiveness
For the way I feel.
I pray for strength, for direction,
For protection, and for salvation
For my entire household, Lord.
I pray for a slower work pace
Which will afford me quality time with my children.

---

[235] Psalm 18:2

[236] Ephesians 2:4; 2 Corinthians 1:3

Above all, Lord, please help me to remember my commitment to You,
As I mature into the person You have called me to be.
In Jesus' name, I pray, Amen.

No. 58
Prayer for a Compassionate Heart

February 13, 1987 (During my personal retreat on Cape Cod, MA)

Praise the LORD, my soul,
and forget not all his benefits—
who forgives all your sins
and heals all your diseases,
who redeems your life from the pit
and crowns you with love and
compassion (Psalm 103:2-4 NIV).

Thank You, Father,
For giving me the opportunities to pray and reflect on my life.
I feel a sense of peace and security,
Knowing that You bear my burdens[237]
And that You answer prayer.[238]
I pray, Holy Spirit,
That You will continually dwell in me
And saturate me with Your presence.
Teach me to be compassionate toward all people.
In Jesus' name, I pray, Amen.

---

[237] Psalm 68:19
[238] Psalm 17:6

No. 59
A Prayer to Love My Neighbor

February 15, 1987 (During my personal retreat on Cape Cod, MA)

If you really keep the royal law found in Scripture,
"Love your neighbor as yourself," you are doing right
(James 2:8 NIV).

Lord, God,
Thank You for the privilege of being Your daughter.
Thank You for opening my eyes to the truth of Your Word,
That I am to love my neighbor as myself;[239]
Loving another is keeping Your commandment.[240]
I pray that I will continue
To love my neighbor as myself.
In Jesus' name, Amen.

---

[239] Matthew 19:19
[240] 1 John 3:23

No. 60
Prayer to Be Revitalized

June 20, 1988 (I went on my personal retreat on Cape Cod, MA; when I returned home, I received my pocketbook, which had been stolen from my home office.)

Though I walk in the midst of trouble, You will revive me;
You will stretch forth Your hand against the wrath of my
enemies, and Your right hand will save me
(Psalm 138:7 NASB).

I worship and praise You this day, Father,
And magnify Your Name,
For You are King of kings and Lord of lords.[241]
You are worthy to be praised.[242]
I give You all the praise, honor,
And glory that belong only to You.[243]
You are the God of miracles.[244]
You are mighty and wonderful,[245]
Merciful, and faithful.[246]

---

[241] Revelation 19:16; 1 Timothy 6:15

[242] Revelation 4:11

[243] Revelation 4:11

[244] Acts 2:22

[245] Isaiah 9:6

[246] Luke 6:36; 1 Corinthians 1:9

You are the potter,
And I am the clay.[247]
I pray that You will mold me,[248]
Fashion me,[249] melt me,
Make me over, pick me up,
And turn my life around.[250]
I pray that You will put my feet on solid ground.[251]

I stand willing and able
To submit to Your will and plan.
Open the door of my heart, Lord.
Take what is not of You and melt it away
And revitalize me,
In the precious name of Jesus,
I pray, Amen.

---

[247] Isaiah 64:8
[248] Job 10:8
[249] Psalm 119:73
[250] Psalm 40:2
[251] Psalm 40:2

No. 61
Prayer for a Clean Heart

May 12, 1990 (On Cape Cod, MA, during a personal retreat while I was experiencing anger and resentment)

Create in me a pure heart, O God,
and renew a steadfast spirit within me
(Psalm 51:10 NIV).

Gracious and loving God,[252]
Forgiver of all sins,[253]
Thank You that I can come
Boldly before Your throne just as I am.[254]
Thank You for Your glorious Gospel,
Which is able to save and restore me.[255]

I acknowledge my sins of anger, resentment, and hatred.
I repent and ask Your forgiveness for all of my sins.
I pray for a clean heart,
In Jesus' name, Amen.

---

[252] Psalm 86:15
[253] Mark 2:7; Psalm 103:3
[254] Hebrews 4:16
[255] Romans 1:16

No. 62
Prayer to Set Priorities

May 19, 1990 (Because there was so much to do in my household, I was asking God to help me establish priorities and organize my life in such a way that I would not be overwhelmed. One priority was having in stock, all the items that I needed for cooking, so I could cook and freeze my dinners for at least five days each week.)

In all your ways acknowledge Him,
And He will make your paths straight (Proverbs 3:6 NASB).

I praise You Lord, God, for giving me a quiet spirit.[256]
Thank You for waking me this morning.[257]
I confess my inability to establish priorities in my life.
I repent of this sin and ask for Your forgiveness.
I pray that You will help me
To determine priorities this day.
In Jesus' name, Amen.

---

[256] Psalm 23:2
[257] Isaiah 50:4

No. 63
Prayer to Increase One's Faith

February 4, 1999 (God was showing me, over the years, how to overcome anger and live a life of faith and trust in Him.)

And without faith it is impossible to please God,
because anyone who comes to him must believe that
he exists and that he rewards those who earnestly seek him
(Hebrews 11:6 NIV).

I come to You, Lord, the ever-present God.[258]
You have never left or forsaken me.[259]
You heal all my diseases.[260]
You are the Comforter of my soul,
The Master of my life,[261]
The faithful and just one,[262]
The forgiver of my sins,[263]
And the bright and morning star.[264]

Sweet, sweet, Jesus, my only friend,[265]
Who hears me when I call,[266]

---

[258] Psalm 46:1
[259] Joshua 1:5
[260] Psalm 103:3
[261] 2 Corinthians 1:3; Luke 17:12-13
[262] Psalm 111:7
[263] Mark 2:7; Psalm 103:3
[264] Revelation 22:16
[265] John 15:13-14
[266] Psalm 17:6; Psalm 86:7

Please help me!
Lord, You know what I am going through.[267]
I pray that You will increase my faith
During these days of trials and tests.
In Jesus' name, Amen.

---

[267] Psalm 139:1-4

No. 64
Prayer When Experiencing Anxiety or Fear

June 28, 1998 (During my personal retreat at Cape Cod, MA, God was dealing with my anxiety over so many things and teaching me that He was my light and my salvation and that I did not need to fear.)

Cast all your anxiety on him because he cares for you (1 Peter 5:7 NIV).

Father, God,
I come to You just as I am.
I confess that I experience anxiety.
I repent of anxiety in Jesus' name.
Your Word says
That You have not given me a spirit of fear but of power.[268]
Forgive me, Lord, for bathing in anxiety.
I pray that You will remove anxiety from my mind.
In Jesus'name, Amen.

---

[268] 2 Timothy 1:7

No. 65
Prayer to Control My Tongue

2010 (God was teaching me to control my tongue.)

....For, "Whoever would love life and see good days must keep their tongue from evil and their lips from deceitful speech (1 Peter 3:10 NIV).

Lord,
I praise and thank You for trials and persecutions,
Because they are tests to strengthen me,
Build my character, patience, endurance, self-esteem,
Hope, faith, and joy. [269]
Most of all, You are building peace,
For You are my peace.[270]

Thank You for keeping me[271]
And compassing me about with a hedge of protection.[272]
Lord, thank You for Your love.[273]
You are my safety net;[274]
Nothing is impossible with You.[275]

---

[269] James 1:2-4; Romans 5:1-5
[270] Ephesians 2:14
[271] Psalm 46:1
[272] Psalm 91:4
[273] Galatians 2:20; Jeremiah 31:3
[274] Psalm 46:1
[275] Mark 10:27

You cause everything to work for my good
And for Your glory, Lord.[276]
Teach me to close the door of my lips
And to be humble at all times.
I pray this in Jesus' name, Amen.

---

[276] Romans 8:28

No. 66
Prayer When Angry

July 6, 1990 (Dealing with family issues)

This you know, my beloved brethren
But everyone must be quick to hear,
slow to speak and slow to anger; for
the anger of man does not achieve the
righteousness of God (James 1:19-20 NASB).

Father,
You have blessed me with life and good health.[277]
I am angry because of the emotional pain that I am experiencing.
Lord, I know You love me;[278]
I am not questioning Your love.
I get impatient waiting on You, Lord.
I confess and ask forgiveness
For my impatience and anger.
Your Word says to be angry and not sin.[279]
I pray that You will deliver me from anger
And that You will teach me to wait patiently on You, Lord.
In Jesus' name, Amen.

---

[277] Psalm 103:3-4
[278] Ephesians 2:4; Jeremiah 31:3
[279] Ephesians 4:26

No. 67
Prayer for Blessings for My Immediate Family

July 31, 1990 (Putting all my needs before God, including asking Him for a part-time job to help with our finances)

Blessed be the God and Father of our Lord Jesus Christ, who has blessed us with every spiritual blessing in the heavenly places in Christ....(Ephesians 1:3 NASB).

Father God,
Thank You for being my daddy.[280]
I entrust You with the care of my children,
Who are Your heritage.[281]
I pray Your blessings upon my family
As well as upon my own life.
I pray that You will guide and protect them, my God.
I pray that You will draw them close to You.
I pray for unity and a bond of peace to permeate my household.
In Jesus' name, Amen.

---

[280] 1 Corinthians 1:3
[281] Psalm 127:3

No. 68
Prayer When Experiencing Unforgiveness

August 28, 1990 (God was teaching me as I became transparent before Him, that He could not forgive my sins if I did not forgive another person's.)

....bearing with one another, and forgiving each other, whoever has a complaint against anyone; just as the Lord forgave you, so also should you (Colossians 3:13 NASB).

Lord, God,
You are great;
You show love to the sinner.[282]
You expect the same of me.
You said, "Vengeance is mine, I will repay."[283]
You also said, Lord, that if I forgive others,
You will forgive me of my sin.[284]
So, Lord, I confess and repent of my unforgiving heart
And ask You to forgive me.
I pray in the name of Jesus, Amen.

---

[282] Ephesians 2:4-6; John 3:16
[283] Romans 12:19
[284] Matthew 6:14

No. 69
Prayer for Strength

September 1, 1990 (I continued to bring all my needs before God, including the need for strength.)

....but those who hope in the LORD
will renew their strength.
They will soar on wings like eagles;
they will run and not grow weary,
they will walk and not be faint
(Isaiah 40:31 NIV).

Lord, God,
You are my strength and my shield.[285]
I pray, Lord, in the name of Jesus,
That You will give me strength
For the battles ahead, Amen.

---

[285] Psalm 28:7

No. 70
Prayer When Feeling Resentful

May 20, 1991 (Feeling resentful from taking on tremendous household and other burdens that left me emotionally drained)

Get rid of all bitterness, rage and anger,
brawling and slander, along with every form of malice
(Ephesians 4:31 NIV).

My Lord and my God,
Thank You for bearing my burdens.[286]
I confess my feeling of resentment.
I repent and ask Your forgiveness for this sin.
I pray, Lord, that I will forego resentment,
In Jesus' name, Amen.

[286] Psalm 68:19

No. 71
Prayer for Peace

May 20, 1991 (I wrote pages of prayers on this day. One of the prayers included a prayer for peace.)

Peace I leave with you; my peace I give you.
I do not give to you as the world gives.
Do not let your hearts be troubled and do not be afraid
(John 14:27 NIV).

Lord God of peace, [287]
I pray that Your peace
Will saturate my heart and mind
And that I will live a life of peace,
In Jesus' name, Amen.

---

[287] Ephesians 2:14; Romans 15:33; 1 Corinthians 14:33

No. 72
Prayer To Be Used of God

October 18, 1991 (Over the years, my journals included many prayer requests. It was time to recognize my gifts and change my requests to "Lord, use me.")

Then David said to his son Solomon, "Be strong and courageous, and act; do not fear nor be dismayed, for the LORD God, my God, is with you. He will not fail you nor forsake you until all the work for the service of the house of the LORD is finished" (1 Chronicles 28:20 NASB).

Father,
Thank You for blessing me with gifts and talents.[288]
I am willing to please You
And to be available to You for the rest of my days.
I pray that You will use me, God, for Your glory.
I bow before You
And pray that I will be saturated with Your love
As I prepare to embrace Your purpose and do Your will,
In Jesus' name, Amen.

---

[288] Ephesians 4:8

No. 73
Prayer to Submit to God's Control

October 28, 1991 (I vacationed with my husband in Rockport, MA; I relaxed, and was able to get a proper perspective on my life.)

If my people, which are called by my name, shall humble themselves, and pray, and seek my face, and turn from their wicked ways; then will I hear from heaven, and will forgive their sin, and will heal their land (2 Chronicles 7:14 KJV).

Lord, God,
I praise and magnify Your Name.
When I am out of control,
You are still in control of my life.[289]
Thank You for carrying me when I am weak.[290]

I confess, repent, and ask for Your forgiveness
For my sins of pride, anxiety, and doubt.
I desire to go where You want me to go
And do whatsoever You will have me to do.
I surrender all to You:
My family, my career, our home, and our financial situation,
And I open the door of my life to You, Lord.

Teach me to be humble and submissive to Your Lordship,
And to rest in You as I await Your provisions.
I submit my life to Your total control,
In Jesus' name, Amen.

---

[289] 2 Corinthians 12:9

[290] Isaiah 46:4

No. 74
Prayer to Trust God

December 10, 1991 (I was aware that God was using my trials to build my character. Because I knew this, I could then trust God for what He was doing in my life.)

Trust in the LORD forever,
for the LORD, the LORD, is the Rock eternal
(Isaiah 26:4 NIV).

Father,
You said in Your Word
That "Those who wait upon the Lord
Shall renew their strength.
They shall mount up with wings like eagles;
They will run and not grow weary.
They will walk and not be faint."[291]
You also promise never to leave or forsake me.[292]
Lord, I have made up my mind to trust You.
I pray that I will continue to trust You in all things,
In Jesus' name, Amen.

---

[291] Isaiah 40:31
[292] Joshua 1:5

No. 75
Prayer for Deliverance

December 10, 1991 (My deliverance included the need to have a pure heart.)

Many are the afflictions of the righteous,
But the LORD delivers him out of them all
(Psalm 34:19 NASB).

Lord God of the Universe,[293]
Who can do exceedingly more than we can ask or think,[294]
Thank You in advance for delivering me
From all of my difficulties,[295] O Holy God.[296]
I am depending on You to pick me up
From the muck and miry clay
And to plant my feet on solid ground.[297]
I pray that You will regard my situation, Lord.
Heal and deliver me by Your Holy Spirit.
I pray these prayers in Jesus' name,
Which is greater than every other name,[298] Amen.

---

[293] Psalm 89:11; Isaiah 42:5
[294] Ephesians 3:20
[295] Psalm 34:4
[296] Psalm 99:5; Isaiah 43:14
[297] Psalm 40:1-3
[298] Philippians 2:9

No. 76
Prayer to Receive God's Anointing to Serve

November 19, 1992 (I was preparing to take the CPA test in Marlboro, MA, to become an accountant, but my father died one day before the test. I brought the needs of many to the Lord, including my immediate family, and asked the Lord to set me apart for the work of ministry.)

....But the anointing which ye have received of him abideth in you, and ye need not that any man teach you: but as the same anointing teacheth you of all things, and is truth, and is no lie, and even as it hath taught you, ye shall abide in him (1 John 2:27 KJV).

Set me apart, dear God, for the work of Your ministry.
I pray that You will anoint my voice, my lips, and my hands.
I pray for the gifts of comfort and healing
With which to bless Your people.
I thank You in advance for Your fresh anointing to serve.[299]
In Jesus' name, Amen.

---

[299] 1 John 2:27

No. 77
Prayer to Be Taught by God

August 31, 1993 (I wanted to be taught by God and not lean on my own understanding.)

The meek will he guide in judgment: and the meek will he teach his way (Psalm 25:9 KJV).

Teach me to wait on You, Lord.
Teach me to love You as You love me.[300]
Teach me to love others as You love me.[301]
Teach me to understand Your purposes for me.
Teach me to press on and not give up.
Teach me to tithe and to give a portion of my income to You.
Teach me, Lord, to set aside time to minister to others.
In Jesus' name, I pray, Amen.

---

[300] Jeremiah 31:3; Ephesians 2:4
[301] Matthew 19:19

No. 78
Prayer to Consecrate One's Life to God

December, 2001 (I spent time with God and consecrated my life to Him.)

....And the very God of peace sanctify you wholly; and I pray God your whole spirit and soul and body be preserved blameless unto the coming of our Lord Jesus Christ (1 Thessalonians 5:23 KJV).

I praise You, today,
My King, my Lord, and my God,[302] forever and ever.
Your grace is sufficient for me.[303]
I recognize that the life that You have given me is a privilege;
I cannot take it for granted.
I desire to live for You for the rest of my days.
Take me and use me; I am Yours.
I pray that You will consecrate my life to You today,
In Jesus' name, Amen.

---

[302] Psalm 24:8; Numbers 15:41

[303] 2 Corinthians 12:9

No. 79
Prayer for Direction

April, 2002 (I submitted my cares, my wants, my every need to God, and asked for His direction.)

The mind of man plans his way,
But the LORD directs his steps
(Proverbs 16:9 NASB).

Father,

I love You with all of my heart and soul. I worship and praise You this day. Lord, I am happy to be Your child.

Thank You for waking me in my right mind.[304] I need not worry or fear, for my life is in Your hands.[305] You are my Master.[306] You promise to supply my every need.[307]

Father, I pray that You will direct and guide me so that my thoughts and actions may be aligned with Your will and purposes for my life. In Jesus' name, Amen.

---

304 Lamentations 3:22-23
305 Acts 17:24-25
306 Luke 17:13
307 Philippians 4:19

No. 80
Prayer of Repentance

May, 2002 (During my stay at a hotel in Lebanon, NH)

Repent ye therefore, and be converted, that your sins may be blotted out, when the times of refreshing shall come from the presence of the Lord (Acts 3:19 KJV).

Father,
I stand before You once again,
Worshipping and loving You, my God.
I am not worthy to stand before You,
But say the word, and my soul shall be healed.[308]
You know all about me,[309] and everything is under Your control.[310]
You are the same God who showed mercy to Your people
When they rebelled against You.[311]
You promised, Lord, that if one repents and turns from one's sins,
That You will heal and restore one to wholeness.[312]
So, I come to You, Lord, confessing and repenting of my sins
And asking for Your forgiveness and restoration,
In Jesus' name, Amen.

---

[308] Matthew 8:8
[309] Psalm 139:1-4
[310] Psalm 66:7
[311] Micah 7:18
[312] 2 Chronicles 7:14

No. 81
Prayer of Obedience

May, 2002 (During my stay at a conference at Grace Church in Lebanon, NH, I was prepared to obey God's commandments and to walk in His ways.)

....He replied, "Blessed rather are those who hear the word of God and obey it" (Luke 11:28 NIV).

Holy God,
Creator of heaven and earth,[313]
King of kings and Lord of lords,[314]
You are my shelter in the time of a storm.[315]
You are my peace,[316] my deliverer,[317]
My Counselor,[318] my rock, and my salvation.[319]
I pay homage to You, Master of the universe.[320]
I magnify Your name, which is highest in the heavens.[321]
I pay my respects to You, Mighty King,[322]
Who is able to do exceedingly more than I can ask or think.[323]

---

[313] Isaiah 45:18; Isaiah 42:5
[314] Revelation 19:16
[315] Psalm 61:3
[316] Ephesians 2:14
[317] Psalm 144:2; Psalm 18:2
[318] Isaiah 9:6
[319] Psalm 18:2; Psalm 62:2
[320] Isaiah 42:5; Psalm 89:11
[321] Philippians 2:9
[322] Psalm 24:8
[323] Ephesians 3:20

Thank You for Your patience with me over the years.[324]
Thank You for leading and guiding me.[325]
I pray that Your light will shine in my life
And that I will continue to live a life of obedience to You,
In Jesus' name, Amen.

[324] Romans 15:5
[325] Psalm 32:8

No. 82
Prayer to Draw Nearer to God

May, 2002 (A day of praising and adoring God for who He is and feeling a desire to leave every detail of my life to His care)

The LORD hath appeared of old unto me, saying,
Yea, I have loved thee with an everlasting love: therefore
with lovingkindness have I drawn thee (Jeremiah 31:3 KJV).

I praise and thank You, God.
You sit mightily on Your throne.[326]
Honor and majesty belong to You, my King,
Who lives forever and ever.[327]
You are the One Who knows all things, sees all things,[328]
Who is, and Who was, and Who is to come,[329]
My Savior,[330] my Redeemer,[331]
My Lord,[332] my Shield,[333] my Counselor,[334] and my Intercessor.[335]

---

[326] Revelation 3:21
[327] Revelation 4:9-11; 1 Timothy 1:17; Jude 1:25; Psalm 5:2
[328] Psalm 139:16
[329] Revelation 1:8
[330] Isaiah 43:3; Numbers 15:41
[331] Isaiah 47:4; Psalm 19:14; Isaiah 44:6; Luke 1:68
[332] Isaiah 43:3; Numbers 15:41
[333] Psalm 28:7
[334] Isaiah 9:6
[335] Hebrews 7:25

Thank You for Your blessed assurance
That all is well with my soul [336]
And that You have everything under Your control.[337]
Thank You for loving me,[338] for giving me joy,[339] for comforting me,[340]
For walking and talking with me,[341]
And for never forsaking me.[342]

Bathe me in Your presence and fill me with Your fresh anointing.
I desire to continually seek You.
I pray that I will draw nearer to You, my Lord,[343]
In Jesus' name, Amen.

---

336 3 John 1:2
337 Psalm 91:4
338 Jeremiah 31:3; Ephesians 2:4
339 Nehemiah 8:10; Jude 1:24
340 2 Corinthians 1:3
341 Psalm 32:8
342 Joshua 1:5
343 Isaiah 43:3; Numbers 15:41

No. 83
Prayer to Live a Life That Pleases God

June, 2002 (During my brief stay with my husband at a hotel in Waltham)

....And do not forget to do good and to share with others,
for with such sacrifices God is pleased (Hebrews 13:16 NIV).

Oh, how much I love You, my God.[344]
I love You from the depths of my heart.
May You be exalted, O God on high,
Who is the lifter of my head.[345]
You are able to do all things
According to the power which works in us.[346]

You have steered the course of my life [347]
And have won all the battles which were raging against me.[348]
Words cannot express my thanks to You for what You have done
And still continue to do for me.
I will continue to rest in You as I run this race,
Looking unto You, Jesus, the Author and Finisher of my faith.[349]

---

[344] Isaiah 43:3; Psalm 18:2; Numbers 15:41
[345] Psalm 3:3
[346] Ephesians 3:20
[347] Psalm 32:8
[348] 2 Chronicles 20:15
[349] Hebrews 12:2

Humble me, God, so that I die to self and live to You.
May my life here on earth be pleasing in Your sight,
O Lord, My Savior and my Redeemer.[350]
I pray in Jesus' name, Amen.

[350] Isaiah 49:26; Psalm 19:14; Luke 1:68

No. 84
Prayer to Overcome Unbelief

July, 2002 (My life was moving in a different direction, and I began to doubt whether I had made the right decision to take a two-year leave of absence from work to help my daughter.)

....Without weakening in his faith, he faced the fact that his body was as good as dead—since he was about a hundred years old—and that Sarah's womb was also dead. Yet he did not waver through unbelief regarding the promise of God, but was strengthened in his faith and gave glory to God, being fully persuaded that God had power to do what he had promised (Romans 4:19-21 NIV).

Lord, my God,[351]
Master of the Universe,[352]
You are the great I AM,[353] my Deliverer,[354]
My Consoler,[355] my Restorer,[356] and my Savior.[357]
I thank You for my situation,
For You have everything under Your control.[358]
I confess, repent, and ask for Your forgiveness
Concerning my unbelief.
I pray that I will live a life of faith
And overcome unbelief,
In Jesus' name, Amen.

---

[351] Numbers 15:41; Isaiah 43:3
[352] Isaiah 42:5; Psalm 89:11
[353] Exodus 3:14
[354] Psalm 144:2; Psalm 18:2
[355] 2 Corinthians 1:3-4
[356] 1 Peter 5:10
[357] Isaiah 43:3; Psalm 18:2; Psalm 144:2
[358] Psalm 66:7

No. 85
Prayer to Overcome Rejection

July 2002, (God showed me that I felt rejected when I could no longer please people or family members to whom I looked for affirmation. It is more important to please God, Who is worthy to be praised, rather than men or women)

For the LORD will not cast off his people, neither will he forsake his inheritance (Psalm 94:14 KJV).

Lord, God,
You are my Master,[359]
And You have a master plan for my life.[360]
I confess my feeling of rejection.
I repent and surrender all of my insecurities to You.
Forgive me, Lord, for my sins.
I pray Lord, that You will help me overcome rejection,
In Jesus' name, Amen.

---

359 Luke 17:12-13
360 Jeremiah 29:11

No. 86
Prayer to Be Guided by the Holy Spirit

July, 2002 (I misplaced my wallet and finally found it on top of the file cabinet.)

But when he, the Spirit of truth, comes, he will guide you into all truth. He will not speak on his own; he will speak only what he hears, and he will tell you what is yet to come (John 16:13 NIV).

I magnify Your Name, God and Father.[361]
Thank You for Your presence,[362]
Your comfort,[363]
And Your strength.[364]
I am able to withstand the storms of life,
For You are with me.[365]
I pray, Holy Spirit, for Your continued guidance,
In Jesus' name, Amen.

---

[361] 1 Corinthians 1:3
[362] Psalm 139:7
[363] 2 Corinthians 1:3
[364] Psalm 18; Psalm 28:7
[365] Psalm 23:4

No. 87
Prayer for Healing

May, 2003 (I attended the Aglow Women's Conference in Natick, MA. I needed prayer for healing.)

....But he was wounded for our transgressions, he was bruised for our iniquities: the chastisement of our peace was upon him; and with his stripes we are healed (Isaiah 53:5 KJV).

I praise and thank You, God, for being my healer.[366]
Your Word states that with Jesus' stripes, I was healed.[367]
I pray, God, that You will heal others
Who need a special healing touch from You.
I pray that You will heal me from ________ (*name the illness*).
I pray for these concerns in Jesus' name, Amen.

---

[366] Exodus 15:26; Psalm 103:3; Psalm 147:3

[367] 1 Peter 2:24

No. 88
Prayer to Have Patience in Suffering

August, 2002 (I continued to suffer emotional pain as I cared for our daughter Jo-An, but God was guiding me and giving me patience in my suffering.)

I waited patiently for the LORD; and he inclined unto me, and heard my cry (Psalm 40:1 KJV).

Lord,
You are the God of all comfort,[368]
And You reign supreme.[369]
Hallowed be thy name, Father.[370]
I bow before You, LORD, Mighty in the heavens and the earth.[371]
I come again to thank You for Your greatness
And to praise You for Your majesty.[372]
I desire to rest at Your feet.
I acknowledge You as my Lord and Savior,[373]
The One who carries my burdens.[374]
The race is not for the swift but for the one who endures to the end.[375]
I am standing on Your Word today, my God, my King.[376]

---

[368] 2 Corinthians 1:3-4
[369] Revelation 19:6
[370] Matthew 6:9
[371] Psalm 150:1; Deuteronomy 3:24
[372] Psalm 48:1; Psalm 93:1
[373] Isaiah 43:3; Luke 2:11
[374] Psalm 68:19; Isaiah 53:4
[375] Ecclesiastes 9:11
[376] Psalm 5:2; Psalm 84:3

I pray, Lord, that You will help me to be patient in suffering
And wait upon You in my worst times,
In Jesus' name, Amen.

No. 89
Prayer to Remove Mountains

September, 2002 (I presented God with all of my mountains, knowing that it takes faith to remove them.)

And Jesus said unto them, Because of your unbelief: for verily I say unto you, If ye have faith as a grain of mustard seed, ye shall say unto this mountain, Remove hence to yonder place; and it shall remove; and nothing shall be impossible unto you (Matthew 17:20 KJV).

Father God,
I worship and praise You this day.
I thank You for faith which is able to move mountains.[377]
I submit all of my mountains to You, God.
I ask You, God, strength of my life,[378] to remove my mountains,
And to remove me out of the way,
So that You can accomplish your work among my family members.
I pray, God, that You will remove the mountain of illness
That prevents me from doing the work that You have called me to do.
Lord, I pray that You will move the mountains of doubt,
Procrastination, and busyness— stumbling blocks
That deter me from accomplishing Your work.
Lord, please remove the mountains of family burdens that I bear.
Lord, show me that only You can shoulder these burdens.[379]

---

[377] Matthew 17:20

[378] Psalm 28:7

[379] Isaiah 53:4; Psalm 68:19

Lord, please tear down the mountains of regrets
That keep me in bondage.
Help me to remember that Jesus died
So that I would not be in bondage to my past
Or be upset about my failures,[380]
But I will live in newness of life.[381]
I pray, Lord, that You will remove these mountains,
In the name of Jesus, Amen.

---

[380] Galatians 5:1; Romans 8:15

[381] Romans 6:4

No. 90
Prayer—Standing in the Gap for Others

November, 2002 (In my daily prayer, I lift up family, friends, and acquaintances who do not know Jesus as their personal Savior.)

And all things, whatsoever ye shall ask in prayer, believing, ye shall receive (Matthew 21:22 KJV).

Father,

Thank You for giving me the opportunity to stand in Your presence, because in Your presence is fullness of joy.[382] I stand in Your presence, not because I am worthy, but on account of the grace I received through Jesus' death on Calvary.[383] Thank You, Lord, for Your grace that is able to save me.[384]

I stand in the gap and pray for friends, acquaintances, and others throughout the world, that You will draw them to Yourself and that they will see You in the midst of their difficulties. I pray these prayers in Jesus' name, Amen.

---

[382] Psalm 16:11; Jude 1:24

[383] Romans 5:8; 2 Timothy 1:9-10

[384] Ephesians 2:8

No. 91
Prayer to Help Others and Use Time for God's Glory

February, 2003 (I am grateful for God's healing in my life both emotionally and physically and would like to use the gifts God has given me to help others.)

Bear one another's burdens, and thereby fulfill the law of Christ (Gal.6:2 NASB).

Lord,
Please remind me that this life I live is not my own.[385]
Because of Your healing power, I am alive today.[386]
I confess and repent of my ingratitude and selfishness,
Wanting every moment for myself.
Help me, dear God, to rise up and help others
The way that You have helped me [387]
And to use time that You have given me, for Your glory.
I pray in Jesus' name, Amen.

---

[385] Jeremiah 10:23; Colossians 3:3

[386] Psalm 103:3; 1 Peter 2:24

[387] Psalm 121:1-2; Hebrews 13:6

No. 92
Prayer before Delivering a Message

June, 2003 (I was part of a panel of speakers at a local church in Boston. Each of us discussed her experiences as a caretaker.)

But he said to me, "My grace is sufficient for you,
for my power is made perfect in weakness."
Therefore I will boast all the more gladly about
my weaknesses, so that Christ's power may rest on me
(2 Corinthians 12:9 NIV).

I honor You this day, God, for You are truly my God.[388]
You are my Spokesman.[389]
You are my Provider,[390]
My Healer,[391]
And my Sustainer.[392]
I pray that You will prepare my heart, Lord,
And assist me in delivering this message before Your people,
In Jesus' name, Amen.

---

[388] Isaiah 43:3; Psalm 18:2
[389] Matthew 10:20; Ezekiel 2:1-2
[390] Philippians 4:19
[391] Exodus 15:26; Psalm 103:3; 1 Peter 2:24
[392] Psalm 55:22

No. 93
Prayer for Deliverance from Guilt

June, 2004 (A simple prayer asking God to deliver me from any unknown sin)

....Let us draw near with a true heart in full assurance of faith, having our hearts sprinkled from an evil conscience, and our bodies washed with pure water (Hebrews 10:22 KJV).

Father,

I have sinned and fallen short of Your glory.[393] I confess guilty feelings for the sins of my past. I repent of the guilt of my past and ask for Your forgiveness, Lord.

I am Your child[394] and Your vessel[395] and feel strongly that I should live as an example of Jesus Christ if I am to win souls for Him. You said if anyone comes to You repenting of his or her sin, You will be faithful to forgive that person and to cleanse him or her from all unrighteousness.[396]

---

393 Romans 3:23
394 1 John 3:1
395 2 Timothy 2:20-21
396 1 John 1:9

I come now, putting my faith and trust in You, my Savior,[397] my Lord,[398] my Anchor, [399] and in Jesus, Who intercedes for me.[400] I pray that You will deliver me from the guilt of my sins, in the name of Jesus Christ, Amen.

---

[397] Isaiah 43:3

[398] Luke 2:11

[399] Hebrews 6:19-20

[400] Romans 8:34

No. 94
Prayer When a Loved One Dies

November, 1992 (My father died.)

Praise be to the God and Father of our Lord Jesus Christ, the Father of compassion and the God of all comfort, who comforts us in all our troubles, so that we can comfort those in any trouble with the comfort we ourselves have received from God (2 Corinthians 1:3-4 NIV).

Lord,

I magnify Your Name this morning, for You said in Your Word that if we are in Christ, whether we live or die, we are Yours.[401]

I remember my father this morning, and I thank You for his life. I grieve for him, Lord, and I miss him dearly, for he made my life full and joyful, and he encouraged me.

I pray, Lord, that You will comfort me during my loss, in the name of Jesus Christ, Amen.

---

[401] Romans 14:8

No. 95
Prayer to Stand on God's Promises

May 29, 2008 (After many years, we were overjoyed that we had found a day habilitation program where Jo-An could receive individual care.)

Your kingdom is an everlasting kingdom, And Your dominion endures throughout all generations (Psalm 145:13 NASB).

My God,[402] my All, my Creator of all good things,[403] the One who comforts me in my afflictions,[404] Who gives me hope when I am experiencing despair,[405] Who never forsakes me and Who loves me unconditionally,[406] I worship and praise You, my God.[407] I hope and trust You in all things.

Please calm the troubled waters as I go through the storms of life. Bring restoration and deliverance to my daughter, Jo-An and peace to my troubled soul. Lord, my daughter needs you right now. Console and rescue her from the trap into which she has fallen. Open her eyes, Lord, so that she can see You in all Your glory. Above all, teach me to stand on Your promises, like Abraham, who believed You, trusted You, and stood on Your promises.[408]
I pray this in Jesus' name, Amen.

---

[402] Isaiah 43:3; Psalm 18:2

[403] Ephesians 3:9; Colossians 1:16

[404] 2 Corinthians 1:3

[405] Romans 15:13

[406] Joshua 1:5; Jeremiah 31:3; Ephesians 2:4

[407] Isaiah 43:3; Psalm 18:2

[408] Romans 4:3; Galatians 3:6

No. 96
Prayer When Weary of Doing Good

April, 2008 (Feeling weary from caring for our daughter Jo-An)

And let us not be weary in well doing: for in due season we shall reap, if we faint not (Galatians 6:9 KJV).

Lord, God,

I can do nothing more. It has already been done. It's Your turn, Father, to take away the trials, the sufferings, and everything that besets me. I am tired of going through the issues in my life. I now lay them down at Your footstool so I can rest. I am tired, Father. I am weary.

Since my life is not my own, I belong to You, and my life is in your hands.[409] I ask You to transform me into the person You would have me be and make me a blessing to others. I pray this in Jesus' name, Amen.

---

[409] Colossians 3:3; Jeremiah 10:23

No. 97
Prayer of Confession

May, 2007 (During my personal retreat on Cape Cod, MA)

I prayed to the LORD my God and confessed and said, "Alas, O Lord, the great and awesome God, who keeps His covenant and lovingkindness for those who love Him and keep His commandments, we have sinned, committed iniquity, acted wickedly and rebelled, even turning aside from Your commandments and ordinances (Daniel 9:4-5 NASB).

Father,

I praise and adore You. I worship and magnify You, O King.[410]

I confess all known and unknown sins, all my secret faults, all areas of my life that are not in conformity to Your will— my thoughts and my actions that deviate from Your statutes, commandments, and ordinances. I repent of those areas, my Lord, God, and I ask for Your forgiveness.

I ask for Your covering and protection. I ask that You hide me in the cleft of Your rock[411] when I am tempted to act or think in a certain sinful way. I pray these prayers in Jesus' name, Amen.

---

[410] Psalm 24:8

[411] Exodus 33:22

No. 98
Prayer to Listen to God's Voice

August, 2009 (Various hospital staff tried to influence us concerning our daughter's future care. I listened to God's voice and brought our daughter home.)

....For he is our God; and we are the people of his pasture, and the sheep of his hand. Today, if ye will hear his voice. (Psalm 95:7 KJV).

Sovereign God over the entire universe,[412] I exalt and magnify Your name.You, Who created the heavens and the earth,[413] You, Who own the cattle on a thousand hills,[414] I love You, because You first loved me.[415]

I pray that Your will shall be done concerning Jo-An, and, Lord, I pray that I will not heed the voices of many, but will heed only Your voice, in Jesus' name, Amen.

---

[412] Deuteronomy 3:24

[413] Isaiah 42:5

[414] Psalm 50:10

[415] 1 John 4:19

Section: 5

Miscellaneous Letters of Prayer

No. 99
Prayer to Know and Walk with Purpose

2010

To everything there is a season,
and a time to every purpose under
the heaven (Ecclesiastes 3:1 KJV).

Father,
Creator of all things[416]
And Master of everything,[417]
I have been wandering for a long time,
Not knowing my purpose in this life.
I rebuke distractions that come my way,
In the name of Jesus.
I am determined to seek Your face, God,
To know my purpose,
And to walk in my destiny.
I pray that You will teach me
To submit to Your authority
And to walk with purpose,
In Jesus' name, Amen.

---

[416] Ephesians 3:9; Colossians 1:16
[417] Luke 17:12-13

No. 100
Prayer for Help to Cease from Complaining

2010

Do all things without murmurings and disputings: That ye may be blameless and harmless, the sons of God, without rebuke, in the midst of a crooked and perverse nation, among whom ye shine as lights in the world (Philippians 2:14-15 KJV).

Father,

I worship and praise You for who You are, the God of heaven and earth.[418] You are so merciful and gracious, loving, and kind to me.[419]

I thank You for my life and for the many blessings that You have bestowed upon me.[420] You guide me every step of the way.[421] You bring me over every stumbling block that comes my way.[422] You redirect my path when I am going in the wrong direction.[423] You continue to give me patience and joy in the midst of my tribulations.[424]

---

[418] Acts 17:24; Isaiah 42:5

[419] Ephesians 2:4-5; Psalm 103:8

[420] Ephesians 1:3

[421] Psalm 32:8

[422] Psalm 34:4

[423] Proverbs 16:9; Psalm 37:23

[424] Colossians 1:11

I repent, God, that I have wasted so much time complaining, when all I had to do was to give You my problems to shoulder. I ask forgiveness for my complaining and pray that I would cease from my decision to complain, in Jesus' name, Amen.

No. 101
Prayer to Know God

2010

My son, if you will receive my words
And treasure my commandments within you,
Make your ear attentive to wisdom,
Incline your heart to understanding;
For if you cry for discernment,
Lift your voice for understanding;
If you seek her as silver
And search for her as for hidden treasures;
Then you will discern the fear of the LORD
And discover the knowledge of God (Proverbs 2:1-5 NASB).

Lord, God,

You made heaven and earth.[425] The skies, the moon, the sun, the clouds, the ocean, the rivers, the mountains, and the entire universe are proof of Your creation.You created light and darkness, rain and snow,[426] man and woman, fish in the sea, birds, and animals of every kind.[427]

---

[425] Isaiah 42:5

[426] Isaiah 45:7; Isaiah 55:10

[427] Isaiah 42:5

I know all about You, but I don't know You in a personal way. My life is in a mess.You say in Your Word that You are a present help in the time of trouble.[428] How can You love someone like me? Yet Your Word says, "For God so loved the world that He gave His only begotten Son, that whoever believes in Him should not perish but have everlasting life."[429]

I have been reading the Bible, but I really don't understand it. Lord, are You there? I'm hurting and need Your touch, God. I pray, Lord God, that You will reach down and help me. I pray that You will take my life and make something of me, Lord God, in Jesus' name, Amen.

---

[428] Psalm 46:1

[429] John 3:16

No. 102
Prayer of Salvation

2010

....That if you confess with your mouth Jesus as Lord, and believe in your heart that God raised Him from the dead, you will be saved (Romans 10:9 NASB).

Lord God of the Universe,
Creator of everything,[430]
I come to You in desperation,
Desiring to have an intimate realtionship with You
And to invite Jesus Christ to be my Lord and Savior.[431]

I confess and repent of my sins
And ask for Your forgiveness.
I accept Jesus as my Lord and Savior,[432]
The One who died on the cross and rose again,
Paying the penalty for my sins,
So I could have salvation and eternal life.[433]
I pray this in Jesus' name, Amen.

---

[430] Colossians 1:16
[431] Isaiah 43:3; Luke 2:11
[432] Isaiah 43:3; Luke 2:11
[433] John 3:16

No. 103
Prayer for the Salvation of My Family

December, 1997

They said, "Believe in the Lord Jesus, and you will be saved, you and your household" (Acts 16:31 NASB).

Father,
You said in Your Word
That I should rest
And wait patiently for You.[434]
I believe that You will bring salvation
To my entire household in Your time.
I pray now, in Jesus' name,
That You will open my family's eyes
To the truth of Your Word
And that they will be willing to receive salvation
And the gift of eternal life.
Amen.

---

[434] Psalm 37:7

No. 104
Prayer for Family Members with Special Needs

2010

I can do all things through Him who strengthens me
(Philippians 4:13 NASB)

Father God,
Creator of heaven and earth,[435]
I worship You for who You are—the Great "I Am."[436]
I thank You for being present in my life[437]
As I deal with the daily issues besetting my
Family Member ____________________.
I know that You love ___________ (*him/her*)
And that there is no partiality with You.[438]
So Father, I pray, humbly submitting to Your will,
That You will bring about peace in ___________ life—
A peace that transcends all understanding,[439]
And that ___________ (*he/she*) will know You in a special way,
As Lord of ___________ (*his/her*)life.

---

[435] Isaiah 42:5; Jeremiah 32:17

[436] Exodus 3:14

[437] Exodus 33:14; Psalm 139:7-8

[438] Romans 2:11

[439] Philippians 4:7

I pray for continued strength
As I advocate on __________ (*name the family member*) behalf.
I pray that I will obtain the support that I need
From the respective governmental agencies
And the school department
Responsible for addressing __________ (*name the family member*) needs.
In Jesus' name, Amen.

No. 105
Prayer for Parents in Divorce or Separation.

2010

....but these have been written so that you may believe that Jesus is the Christ, the Son of God; and that believing you may have life in His name (John 20:31 NASB).

Holy God,[440] loving Father,[441]
I worship and praise You, mighty God.[442]I praise You for who You are.

I thank You for loving a person like me, even with all my faults. You said that nothing can separate me from Your love.[443]

I confess and repent of guilt, anger, and bitterness and ask for Your forgiveness. I surrender all to You and present my body as a living sacrifice, holy and acceptable to You.[444]

I pray that You will help and guide me in the coming years to live anew. In Jesus' name, Amen.

---

[440] Psalm 99:5
[441] Ephesians 2:4; John 3:16
[442] Deuteronomy 10:17
[443] Romans 8:38-39
[444] Romans 12:1

No. 106
Prayer for a Parent of a Rebellious Child/Teen

2010

....But the fruit of the Spirit is love, joy, peace, longsuffering, gentleness, goodness, faith.... (Galatians 5:22 KJV).

Holy and righteous God,[445]

Who has the divine power to pull down strongholds,[446] I praise and worship You today and thank You for bringing me this far by faith, leaning on Your everlasting arms.[447]

I confess and repent of anger, bitterness, or resentment that I have harbored, and I ask You to forgive me of these sins.

I pray for patience and love as I discipline my child __________. You said, Lord God, that nothing is impossible with You.[448] I pray for ___________ that ___________(*he/she*) will change ___________ (*his/her*) behavior, that___________ (*he/she*) will be subjected to Your will and purpose, and that ___________ (*he/she*) will be obedient to me ___________ (*his/her*) parent. In Jesus' name, Amen.

---

445 Psalm 145:17

446 2 Corinthians 10:4

447 Ephesians 2:8; Deuteronomy 33:27

448 Mark 9:23; Mark 10:27

No. 107
Prayer for Grandchildren

2010

If ye abide in me, and my words abide in you, ye shall ask what ye will, and it shall be done unto you (John 15:7 KJV).

I love You, Lord, for You have answered my prayers[449] and have blessed me with grandchildren.

I pray for my grandchildren and ask, Lord,
that You bless them with good health and strength
and that You protect them from harm. I also pray that my
grandchildren will grow in the knowledge of Your ways
and will accept Jesus as Lord and Savior.
In Jesus' name, Amen.

---

[449] Psalm 17:6; Psalm 86:7

No. 108
Prayer for a Victim/Family of the Victim

2010 (Includes bribery, child abuse or neglect, child molestation, domestic violence, deceit, fear, gang violence, incest, murder, pornography, perjury, or any type of crime)

Fear not, for you will not be put to shame;
And do not feel humiliated, for you will not be disgraced;
But you will forget the shame of your youth,
And the reproach of your widowhood
you will remember no more.
For your husband is your Maker,
Whose name is the Lord of Hosts....
(Isaiah 54:4-5 NASB).

Lord, God of all comfort,[450] who cares for all, even for those who have been victimized,[451] I confess that I am ____________________ (*a victim/ a family member of the victim*) of __________ (*name the crime*).

I confess feelings of fear, anxiety, anger, unforgiveness and bitterness that I experience from day to day because of my pain. I repent of these feelings, Father.

I pray that You will forgive me of these feelings and deliver me from the bondage of my past. I forgive __________ (*name the person*), who is responsible for my pain. Please come into my heart, dear God. Take my life and turn it around for Your glory. I pray in Jesus' name, Amen.

---

[450] 2 Corinthians 1:3

[451] 1 Peter 5:7

No. 109
Prayer for a Family Member Who Is Imprisoned

2010

Hear my cry, O God;
listen to my prayer.
From the ends of the earth I call to you,
I call as my heart grows faint;
lead me to the rock that is higher than I (Psalm 61:1-2 NIV).

Father,

I bless and magnify Your name. I will continue to praise You for as long as I live.

Thank You, Father, for keeping __________ (*name your family member*) safe.[452] You said that when I call on You in trouble, that You will hear and answer my prayers, [453] so I am standing on Your promises today.

I pray that __________ (*name your family member*) will repent of __________(*his/her*) sins and give__________ (*his/her*) life to You. I pray that You will give me the endurance that I need as I struggle to deal with __________ (*name your family member*) situation. In Jesus' name, Amen.

---

[452] Psalm 27:5; Psalm 91:4

[453] Psalm 17:6

No. 110
Prayer for a Family Member Facing Street Life

2010

These things I have spoken to you, so that in Me you may have peace. In the world you have tribulation, but take courage; I have overcome the world" (John 16:33 NASB).

Holy Father,
I exalt You and give You the highest praise.
You said praises are comely for the righteous.[454]
I come into Your presence because in Your presence is fullness of joy.[455]
Thank You for hearing my prayers.[456]

You know the situation I face.[457]
My family member _________, is _______________________.
I have tried continually to give _____(*him/her*) advice,
But____(*he/she*) is not obeying me.
I pray not only for _____(*him/her*),
but for ______(*his/her*) friends, Lord,
That they will change their lives and live anew, in Jesus' name.

---

[454] Psalm 147:1
[455] Psalm 16:11
[456] Psalm 86:7; Psalm 17:6
[457] Psalm 139:1-4

Lord, I pray for a miracle that somehow, somewhere,
You will make Yourself known to ________ (*name your family member*).
I pray for protection for _____(*him/her*)
As _____(*he/she*) makes decisions to turn _________(*his/her*) life around.
In Jesus' name, Amen.

No. 111
Prayer for a Parent Who Has Lost a Child

2010

I will lift up my eyes to the mountains;
From where shall my help come?
My help comes from the LORD,
Who made heaven and earth (Psalm 121:1-2 NASB).

Father God,
You are my God.[458]
You are Sovereign over every person, place, and thing.[459]
You sent Your Son, Jesus Christ, to die on the cross,
And because of Your grace, I have access to You, Father.[460]

You know everything about me.[461]
I feel lost without __________ (*name your son/daughter*)
Who died from______________________.
__________ (*name your son/daughter*) meant so much to me.
__________(*He/She*) was a wonderful child.
__________(*He/She*) didn't deserve this, Lord.
I feel sad, lonely, and angry because of my loss.

---

458 Psalm 18:2
459 Acts 4:24
460 Ephesians 2:15-18
461 Psalm 139:1-4

I confess and repent of my feelings
And ask for Your forgiveness.

I pray that You will renew my spirit
And give me a new start,
In Jesus' name, Amen.

No. 112
Prayer When Faced with Natural Disasters

2010

Blessed are they that mourn: for they shall be comforted (Matthew 5:4 KJV).

God,
You are Holy[462] and the Creator of this entire universe.[463]
You spoke, and the world and everything was created.[464]
You are still God, even with my loss,
So, I thank You for saving and preserving me.[465]
Lord, I have lost everything and have lost loved ones,

_________________________.
I have nowhere to go and have nothing to eat or drink.
Father, I confess and repent of my rebellious ways,
And I ask Your forgiveness for people in my _________ (*country/state*).
I submit to Your Lordship
And make a conscious decision to obey You.

---

[462] Psalm 99:5
[463] Isaiah 42:5; Colossians 1:16
[464] Isaiah 42:5; Colossians 1:16
[465] Psalm 121:8; Psalm 37:28

You said all things work together for good.[466]
I pray, Lord God, in Jesus' name,
That You will cause people in various nations
To have compassion, understand our need,
And send help to rebuild the _____ (*country/state*) of
_________,
And to help the people of _______, Amen.

---

[466] Romans 8:28

No. 113
Prayer to Overcome Fear of Air Travel

2010

There is no fear in love; but perfect love casts out fear, because fear involves punishment, and the one who fears is not perfected in love (1 John 4:18 NASB).

Lord of the skies and Lord over everything,[467]
I thank You for this opportunity
To travel to ____________________.
I confess my fears about traveling
And repent of every fear.
I ask Your forgiveness for being afraid,
For You said that there is no fear in love
And that perfect love casts out fear, for fear is torment.[468]
I bring every thought captive.
I pray that I will enjoy the flight,
In Jesus' name, Amen.

---

[467] 1 Chronicles 29:11

[468] 1 John 4:18

No. 114
Prayer for One's Marriage

2010

Love is patient, love is kind and is not jealous; love does not brag and is not arrogant, does not act unbecomingly; it does not seek its own, is not provoked, does not take into account a wrong suffered, does not rejoice in unrighteousness, but rejoices with the truth; bears all things, believes all things, hopes all things, endures all things (1 Corinthians 13:4-7 NASB).

Father,

Thank You for blessing me with _________ (*name your spouse*).[469]

I pray in Jesus' name that I will continue to love _________ (*name your spouse*) in the way that I loved _________ (*him/her*) before we were married. Help me to take Your covenant of marriage seriously and to realize that I can do all things through Christ who gives me strength.[470] Amen.

---

[469] Ephesians 1:3

[470] Philippians 4:13

No. 115
Prayer for a Single Man or Woman

2010

Delight yourself in the LORD;
And He will give you the desires of your heart (Psalm 37:4 NASB).

Father,
Please give me the patience to wait for the right person
Whom You have already provided for me.
Whatever is Your will for me,
I pray that I will understand Your will for my life
And walk according to Your calling and direction,
In Jesus' name, Amen.

No. 116
Prayer When Dealing with Lust, Adultery/Other

2010 (Other includes sins of pride, envy, jealousy, discord, selfishness, dissentions, and sexual immorality as stated in Galatians 5:19)

You, dear children, are from God and have overcome them, because the one who is in you is greater than the one who is in the world (1 John 4:4 NIV).

Father,
I have sinned and fallen short of Your glory.[471]
I confess and repent of my _________ (*sin/sins*)
of _________________.
I pray that You will forgive me, Father,
for my _________ (*sin/sins*),
In Jesus' name, Amen.

---

[471] Romans 3:23

No. 117
Prayer for the Mentally Challenged

2010 (This represents an incomplete list of disorders which includes schizophrenia, bipolar, depression, personality, and eating.)[472]

....If the Son therefore shall make you free, ye shall be free indeed (John 8:36 KJV).

Father,
God of heaven and earth,[473]
I worship and praise You this day.
I desire to sit and be nurtured at Your feet.
I confess and repent of the sins of my past generations
And also for the person who has brought about my pain.
I ask You to forgive them, Lord, for their sins.
I also ask forgiveness for any bitterness and anger
That I may have harbored.
I rebuke ___________ (*name the disorder*)
And cast it out of my mind and body to the dry places,
In the name of Jesus Christ.
I declare that I am healed and set free
By the blood of Jesus, Amen.

---

[472] "List of mental disorders." Available from Http://en.wikipedia.org/wiki/List_of_mental_disorders_as_defined _by_the _DSM_ and_ICD. Accessed 26 March 2011

[473] Isaiah 42:5

No. 118
Prayer for the Chemically Dependent/Other

2010 (Other addictions include alcohol, food, sex, and activity related addictions such as gambling, casino gambling, and web surfing.)[474]

Now unto him that is able to keep you from falling, and to present you faultless before the presence of his glory with exceeding joy.... (Jude 1:24 KJV).

My God, who has spoken in these last days by Your Son, Jesus,[475]
I praise and worship You, Father.
I confess and repent of my sin of _________.
I ask Your forgiveness for my sin
And determine to live a life dependent on You, my God.[476]
In Jesus' name, I pray, Amen.

---

474 "Different types of addictions." Available from Http: www.differenttypesofaddicion.com/?p=21. Accessed 26 March 2011.

475 Hebrews 1:2

476 Psalm 5:2

No. 119
Prayer of Hope

2010 (For family members, friends, our nation, world peace, Government officials, educators, body of Christ, justice, and other prayer needs)

Praise be to the God and Father of our Lord Jesus Christ!
In his great mercy he has given us new birth into a living
hope through the resurrection of Jesus Christ from the dead...
(1 Peter 1:3 NIV).

Father,
You are my hope, [477]
And Your hope does not make me ashamed
Because of Your love
That is shed abroad in my heart by the Holy Ghost. [478]
I pray in Jesus' name,
That I will allow Your Word to saturate my heart and mind
And that I will live in hope for ___________ (*name the person/country/condition/situation*), Amen.

---

[477] 1 Timothy 1:1

[478] Romans 5:5

Subject Index

Subject Index

Subject Index

Subject Index